Contents

Look up the bold words in the glossary
on page 32 of this book.

What are tropical rainforests?

Tropical rainforests are forests that grow close to the **equator** – in the **tropics**.

Over half the world's **species** of animals and plants are squeezed into this narrow band of land each side of the equator.

However, the rainforests are also home to an increasing number of people.

Tropical rainforests are some of the last untouched forests on the Earth. In some rainforests trees stretch over thousands of kilometres.

However, all rainforests, both large and small, are under threat from people...

Rainforest trees grow so close together you cannot see down to the ground.

What the rainforest looks like from a riverside.

Exploring the endangered rainforest

SECOND EDITION

An Asian elephant, whose home is the rainforest.

Dr Brian Knapp

Beautiful – but endangered

This is a jaguar, a forest floor hunter of the South American rainforests. It can be 2 m long and a metre tall at the shoulder. The rough blotches (they are not true spots) make the jaguar harder to see while it waits among the trees to ambush its prey.
It has specially padded paws to help it move silently on the forest floor. Jaguars mainly hunt at night using their excellent eyesight. There may be only 15,000 jaguars alive in the wild today. A jaguar is just one of many animals and plants endangered by the thoughtless activities of people.

Did you know… ?

- Rainforests are found within 10°N and 10°S of the equator.

- Tropical rainforests are the oldest forests in the world.

- Tropical rainforests have more species of trees than any other part of the world.

- Tropical rainforest trees have broad leaves.

- Rainforest trees shed their leaves at different times, so some might be leafless whilst others are in full flower.

- Rainforest trees do not touch, but are separated from one another by a metre or so – look again to prove it!

This map shows areas of rainforest in green. The biggest rainforest surrounds the River Amazon in Brazil, South America. The other huge rainforest is near the River Congo in West Africa. In Asia the largest area of rainforest stretches from Thailand right across Indonesia. Australia also has a small area of rainforest in Queensland.

 Which continent has the most rainforest?

The weather

It is always hot, usually windless near the ground (even if it is very windy above the trees) and very sticky – **humid**.

Rain falls each day in nearly every month of the year.

An afternoon view from a hut in Thailand, just after the rainstorms have finished.

Early morning mist over a rainforest in Venezuela.

A year's weather in a rainforest:

January	February	March	April	May	June
26°	 26°	26°	26°	26°	 26°

If you walk in the rainforest you will rarely see the Sun, for giant trees reach high above you and shade out the ground almost completely.

Did you know… ?

- Most tropical rainforests get at least 2 m of rain a year.

- Because it rains so often, rainforest plants have no protection from **drought**.

- Hot, sticky weather means that people feel comfortable with few clothes on. The weather also makes people tired and want to sit around all day.

- Rainforests do not have hot and cold seasons like us. It is hot all of the time.

- The weather is the same on most days all year: the sky begins clear, with mists hanging over the forest tops. After a sunny morning, clouds form, claps of thunder are heard and torrential rainshowers begin. Then, as the Sun sets, the rain stops and the sky clears.

Q How much rain falls in your part of the world?

July	August	September	October	November	December
27°	27°	28°	28°	27°	27°

A forest of many layers

In a rainforest it is hot, rainy and there is lots of sunlight. These are ideal conditions for all plants, and trees grow fast and reach great heights.

Almost all rainforest trees are like natural umbrellas. They have long, straight trunks. Near the top of a tree, the trunk suddenly divides into many branches like the spokes of an umbrella. This is where all of the leaves occur.

A rainforest has many trees of similar heights. Most fully-grown trees are about 30 m tall. Their leaves spread out and make a **canopy** that shades the ground below.

Just a few **emergent** trees rise up, or emerge, from the canopy to 50 m.

Below the canopy are some smaller trees (we call them **understory** trees). Many of them are simply waiting their turn to grow up when the canopy trees die of old age.

Q What is 'the canopy'?

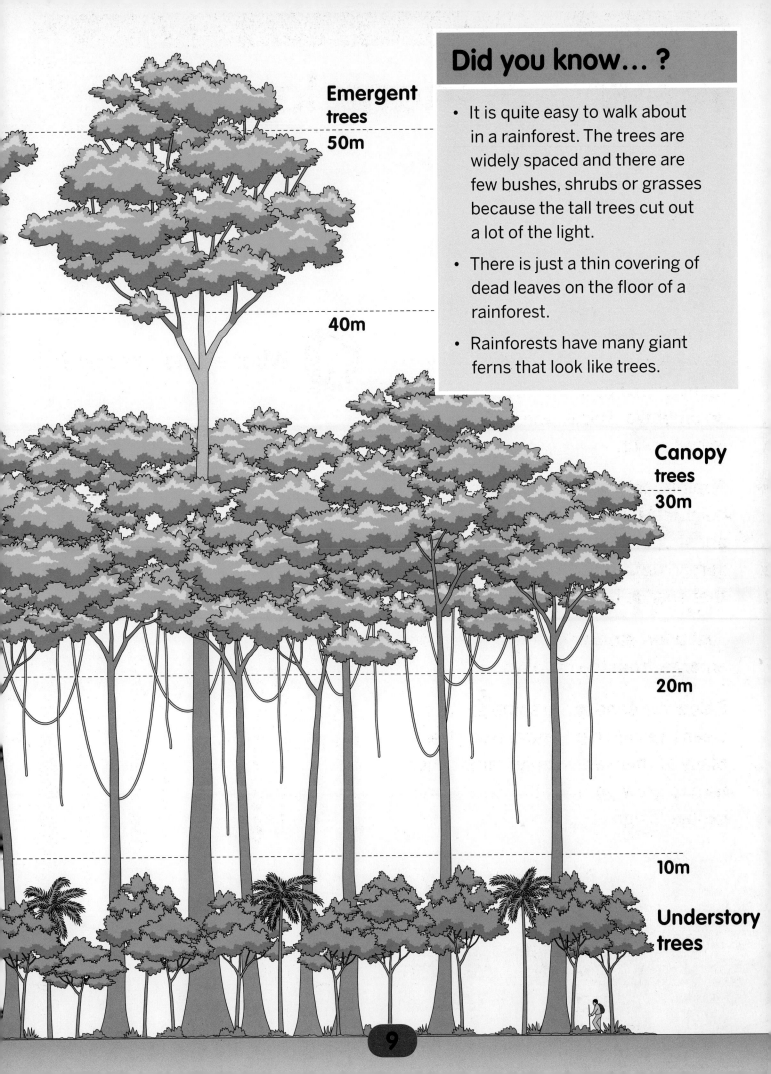

Emergent trees

50m

40m

Canopy trees

30m

20m

10m

Understory trees

Did you know… ?

- It is quite easy to walk about in a rainforest. The trees are widely spaced and there are few bushes, shrubs or grasses because the tall trees cut out a lot of the light.

- There is just a thin covering of dead leaves on the floor of a rainforest.

- Rainforests have many giant ferns that look like trees.

What lives in a rainforest?

Rainforests are home to half of all the kinds (species) of living animals and plants on the Earth.

These species live together and depend on each other. This is why, if one is destroyed, many other species might also die.

To begin with, everything depends on the plants. They make the new leaves, nectar, pollen and flowers that many creatures eat. In turn, hunting animals feed on the plant-eaters. Then, when creatures and plants die, and fall to the forest floor, there are yet more animals waiting to eat the remains.

Sloth

Parrot

Howler monkey

Angels trumpets

Hummingbird

Small leaf tamarind

Leaf-cutter ant

Jaguar

Harpy eagle

Vulture

Emerald tree boa

Morpho butterfly

Bird of paradise

Red-eyed tree frog

Flying fox

Green iguana

Dung beetle

Millipede

Pill beetle

Q What do we call creatures that come out (a) in the night and (b) in the day?

Did you know... ?

- All living things need energy to live. Each time something is eaten about a tenth of the energy it used to live is passed on as food. This means that there can be only a tenth as many meat eaters (like jaguars) as plant eaters (like wild boar). This is why hunting animals are far less common than plant eaters.

- You rarely see an animal of any kind when you walk about in a rainforest because most animals live near the tree tops, some are **camouflaged** and so are hard to spot, and many more only come out at night.

- Because all animals depend on plants, if the trees are cut down and not replaced, many animal species will die, too.

The secrets of trees

Trees need sunlight to grow and make their leaves, branches and trunks. That is why big trees only have leaves at the top (the crown).

The small trees near the ground have very large leaves to gather in all the light in dim conditions. If they grow into big trees and reach the sunshine of the canopy they will lose these big leaves and grow a new set of smaller ones.

Many leaves are hard and shiny and have tips that allow rainwater to drip off easily after rain stops. Without it, mould would quickly grow over the leaves.

Q **What sort of bark and leaves do the trees near you have?**

Many trees have ribs near the ground. These are called buttresses. They look as if they are holding the tree up, but they are not; they are simply the roots spreading out into the ground.

Did you know... ?

- Tropical rainforest trees have incredibly thin bark – just a couple of millimetres.

- The bark of many trees is very smooth.

- Some trees have thorns on their trunks.

Guests and stranglers

In a rainforest, many plants use each other to get to the sunlight.

Some plants grow on the branches of trees. They include orchids and bromeliads. They use the **nourishment** in the rain that falls on to their leaves and do no harm to the tree.

The 'natural ropes' that hang from tree branches are actually the stems of woody climbing plants such as vines. They are called lianas.

A few plants, however, eventually strangle the trees that support them.

This strangler fig began as a tiny, sticky seed left in animal droppings high in a tree. As the fig grew it sent thin roots snaking down the trunk of the tree which dug into the soil. The fig then grew lots of leaves, smothering and killing the tree that supported it.

Did you know... ?

- You can find rainforest bromeliads and orchids in a garden centre.

- Some guest trees – even stranglers – are very important to animals. In some forests nearly three quarters of all animals depend on the sweet fruits of the fig – a strangler tree.

- The lianas give easy ways for animals like lemurs, sloths and monkeys to get between trees, so they never have to come down to the ground.

Rainforest orchids.

Bromeliads

Q Some plants look like ropes hanging in the forest. What is their real name?

High flyers in the canopy

Most rainforest flowers and fruits are found in the canopy, but the canopy trees do not touch. Everything that lives in the canopy must be able to get across the gaps between trees, so most high canopy creatures can fly.

Insects take pollen and nectar from the flowers. Birds eat the insects, sip the flower nectar and eat the fruits.

At night, bats fly about eating fruit or hunting for night-flying insects.

Toucans are examples of birds found only in one area of rainforest – Central America. Because they are found in just one place they are easily endangered.

Did you know...?

- Canopy trees have more flowers and fruits than any other trees in the world. This is why they can provide food for so many animals.

- Most of the animals of the rainforest are insects.

- A quarter of all the world's insect species live here. For example, there are nearly 500,000 kinds of beetles.

Many parrots are green, a good camouflage colour. You can hear them but not see them in the rainforest canopy. But some are bright red and so are easier to spot. Many brightly-coloured parrot species are endangered due to deforestation and the illegal pet trade.

A flying fox.

The Atlas moth is the world's largest moth, with a wingspan of about 30 cm.

Hummingbirds are some of the tiniest birds, weighing just a few grams. They beat their wings at up to 80 times a second and can hover close to a flower while they sip at its nectar.

A rainforest butterfly. This type is called a longwing.

Swinging and gliding – for how long?

Below the high canopy, tree ferns, palms, native bananas and many other fruits grow. Lianas also hang between the branches.

This is the home of many well-known animals, including monkeys, snakes and lizards.

All of these animals have special arms, fingers, toes and tails that let them move about between the branches and the liana rope stems without ever coming down to the ground. However, they need special trees to eat from and they can't survive if we cut down the forests.

An orang-utan (which means "person of the forest" in Malay) feeds only on a small number of tree types. Many things sold in the world are made from ramin, an Asian rainforest wood whose trees provide the main food for the orang-utan. This is why it is endangered.

Monkeys and chimpanzees are superb movers, but they are not common any more. The rarest is the spider monkey – there are just 50 pairs known in the wild! The spider monkey only eats special fruits and 80 per cent of the rainforest that it depends on for food has been destroyed.

Lemurs are one of the most endangered of animals because they are found naturally only on the island of Madagascar (Africa). They mainly eat a variety of fruits, flowers and leaves as well as insects, spiders and small lizards.

Sloths live upside down in South America and Central America. They have special claws that let them hang onto branches. The leaves they eat do not have much energy in them, but by moving very slowly they use very little energy.

Q What do monkeys use their tails for?

Near the forest floor

Very little of the rainforest's sunlight reaches the forest floor, so only a few plants can grow there. Many animals rely on gathering fruits that fall from the trees above.

Elephants and rhinos are two of the large animals that move about on the open floor, snuffling up fruits, but it is home to boars, buffalo, frogs and snakes, too.

Wild boar.

Q **Why are so many forest floor animals green?**

Boas and pythons can grow to 6 m. They are constrictors. They do not have venom in their fangs to kill prey; instead, they wrap coils of their body around their victims (birds and other small animals) and squeeze each time the animal breathes out. Eventually the prey suffocates. They swallow their prey whole, and take several days or even weeks to digest it. This is an emerald tree boa.

Did you know…?

- Elephants are the largest animals found in the rainforest. Rainforest elephants are found in Asia (the home of African elephants is grassland). Asian elephants are plant-eaters, feeding on leaves, bamboo, grasses, vines, tender shoots, bark and fruit.

Chameleons are a form of lizard. They can change their colour to match whatever they are standing on. Their mouths contain long, sticky tongues that they whip in and out to catch their food, which is mainly insects.

Frogs are meat-eaters, feeding mainly at night on anything that will fit inside their mouths, such as moths and flies. Tree frogs have feet like suction cups which help them to hold on to leaves, branches and the trunks of trees. This is a green tree frog.

The most famous rainforest frog is the red-eyed tree frog.

Close to the soil

Rainforest trees grow tall, and so you would think the soil they grow in would be very fertile. But the rainforest soil is old. It is so old that nearly all of the goodness has been used up or washed away. Because of this rainforest plants cannot rely on the soil for their food. Instead, they have to make use of what dies for their food.

Small animals also keep a look out for any leaves they drop, for they are food to them, too.

Giant millipedes up to 30 cm long roam the forest floor looking for dead leaves to eat. Their brown colour is camouflage.

Did you know… ?

- The tallest trees have roots that only go 50 cm into the soil because there is no nourishment for them below this.

- Termites (white ants) are expert at eating dead wood. Wood is made of an important food – sugar. Termites are very important in a rainforest because no other insect can eat the wood of trees.

Armies of ants move across the forest in vast numbers. These leaf-cutter ants are the only animals (other than humans) to cultivate their own food from fresh leaves. Leafcutter ants can carry almost ten times their own weight back to their underground nests where the leaves are chewed into a pulp and used to grow fungus. The ants eat the fungus; they do not eat the leaves.

Q **Why is the rainforest soil so poor?**

Jungle

A natural rainforest is NOT the same as a jungle. A jungle is a tangle of plants all fighting for sunlight because something unusual has destroyed the big trees and let the light in.

It is easy to walk among the big trees of a rainforest. It is almost

Did you know… ?

- The word jungle comes from the Persian word *jangal*, meaning uncultivated land that had once been used by people.

- Areas of jungle are increasing because people tamper with the rainforest, for example, by taking out the large trees for timber.

impossible to cut your way through the tangle of small stems in a jungle.

Jungles can occur naturally, for example, if a large tree falls and knocks down others. But most jungles are caused by people cutting down the large trees and carrying them away for timber.

Native hunters using bows and arrows in open ground. Mostly, however, they use the bows to bring down monkeys from the forest trees, or catch boar running on the forest floor. They could not do this in a jungle.

Q **Why can't we call all rainforests jungles?**

Slash and burn

Few people live in a rainforest. The wildlife mainly lives high in the trees and is hard to catch. Few plants are suitable for people to eat.

The soil has little nourishment for crops. This is why, for thousands of years, native peoples have had to cut down patches of forest, let the trees dry and then burn them so they can use the ashes. Seeds of maize or some other crop grow in the ashes, not the soil.

Crops will grow well in ashes for a few years until the goodness in the ashes is used up. Then the people have to move on and burn another area.

It takes more than a century for the trees of the rainforest to regrow again. So just a few people can change a large area of forest.

An area of forest being burned. You can still see the flames licking across the ground. The fire has swept past the standing tree, leaving it almost unburned.

This is a small area in the rainforest that has been cleared by tribespeople for their homes. You can still see the stumps of the trees that were cut and burned.

Q **What do people grow their crops in?**

Using the rainforest

Today many people try to use the rainforest. In Asia, for example, many areas have now been ploughed and used for rice. In South America the rainforest is cut down, maize or grass sown and cattle grazed.

Many more people cut down the trees and ship them out to foreign countries to use the wood.

Some rainforest trees produce useful crops. Bananas, rubber and palm oil are just some important examples. In many areas the rainforest is cut down to grow these trees as crops.

Many food plants grow in a rainforest, but in nature they are widely scattered. In a tree farm, the rainforest is cut down and the food trees grown in rows. The food trees grow well because they are natural rainforest trees. The picture shows oil palm trees.

The forest contains many valuable hardwood trees. The wood can be used for furniture and flooring.

Rice is not a rainforest plant (it originally came from the foothills of the Himalaya). But it will grow in any warm waterlogged soil.

Flat land close to rivers also has enough nourishment to grow crops year after year. So, in South East Asia, in particular, huge areas of rainforest have been cut down and the land used for rice (called rice paddies). See how the forest remains on the hills behind.

Did you know… ?

- All of these foods come from rainforests: Bananas (background picture), yams, avocados, pineapples, peppers, peanuts, oranges, papayas, lemons, pepper, coconuts, sugarcanes, cassava and cacao (chocolate), coffee beans, cashews, nutmegs, cinnamon, chicle (used in chewing gum), vanilla and Brazil nuts.

Q **Why is the rainforest being cut down?**

Help save the rainforest

Be an eco-tourist, visit a rainforest

People are cutting down their own rainforests because they need to make a living, just like you and me. If we went on holiday to the rainforest areas, to see animals and trees, then rainforest people would make more money from guiding us and giving us places to stay, than by cutting down the trees. So they would be able to look after the rainforest and make a decent living.

Where would you like your family to go on holiday?

Look up rainforest holidays on the Internet (type in 'Rainforest Holiday' and search). Make sure they are eco-friendly tours. Think up 10 questions you might ask to tell if your eco-lodge is really an eco-lodge (rather than just pretending), for example, do the local people work in the lodge?

Watch a rainforest grow

- Choose two or three small plants that your local garden centre tells you grow in a tropical rainforest.

- Put a thin layer of sand and gravel at the bottom of a pot, then add potting compost and your plants. Press down firmly so the soil is just below the pot rim.

- Place three small canes in the pot around the edges.

- Water the plot.

  - Place a large plastic bag over the pot and tuck the edges inside the pot. Keep your rainforest warm and out of direct sunlight.

  - In a couple of days you should see moisture form inside the bag. This moisture has been released by the plants and will fall down onto the soil and find its way into the plant through the roots.

- Now you have a rainforest which will last for many months without any attention.

Eat rainforest food

Make a food basket of rainforest foods:

- Collect these from your supermarket and then make a nice display of them in a basket:

  Bananas, yams, avocados, pineapples, peppers, peanuts, oranges, papayas, lemons, pepper, coconuts, sugar canes, cassava and cacao (chocolate), coffee beans, cashews, nutmegs, cinnamon, chicle (used in chewing gum), vanilla and Brazil nuts.

- Take a picture and label it for a classroom display.

Help care for the rainforest

Do not buy goods that are not from well managed forests. If you buy things of wood, look to see if it is a tropical wood. Does the seller guarantee the wood comes from a rainforest where more trees are planted to replace those taken away? If the seller cannot guarantee this, and show you a piece of paper with the guarantee written on, then **DON'T BUY IT**. That way, you will have done your bit for the rainforest.

Q Can you find three ways in which YOU can help save the tropical rainforest?

Glossary

buttress A triangular shape of root that seems to be propping up the main stem.

camouflage To take on the colour or pattern of the surroundings so that an animal cannot easily be seen.

canopy The uppermost part of the forest, made up of the crowns of the big trees.

continent A very large area of land. The continents are: Africa, Antarctica, Asia, Australia, Europe, North America and South America.

deforestation Taking away large areas of forest and using the land for something else.

drought An unusually long time without rain.

emergent A tree that rises above its surroundings.

endangered At risk from being wiped out as a species.

equator The line around the Earth half way between the poles.

humid Air that has so much moisture in it that the air feels sticky.

nourishment A word for the energy in food.

species A group of living things that can breed together.

tropics The lands either side of the equator in which it is more or less evenly hot all year.

understory The group of smaller trees that grow under the main rainforest giants.

Index

Curriculum Visions

Curriculum Visions Explorers
This series provides straightforward introductions to key worlds and ideas.

You might also be interested in
'Rainforest life', an extended edition of this book with a 64pp extent, plus 'Exploring rainforest people' and 'Exploring the threatened oceans' in the Explorer series. Additional notes in PDF format are also available from the publisher. All of these products are suitable for KS2.

There's much more online including videos
You will find multimedia resources covering life in the rainforest as well as others in geography, history, religion, MFL, maths, music, spelling and more at:

www.CurriculumVisions.com

(Subscription required)

A CVP Book
This second edition © Atlantic Europe Publishing 2014

First edition 2007. First reprint 2008.

The right of Brian Knapp to be identified as the author of this work has been asserted by him in accordance with the Copyright, Designs and Patents Act 1988.

All rights reserved. No part of this publication may be reproduced, stored in a retrieval system, or transmitted in any form or by any means, electronic, mechanical, photocopying, recording or otherwise, without prior permission of the copyright holder.

Author
Brian Knapp, BSc, PhD
Educational Consultant
JM Smith (former Deputy Head of Wellfield School, Burnley, Lancashire); the Librarians of Hertfordshire School Library Service
Senior Designer
Adele Humphries, BA, PGCE
Editor
Gillian Gatehouse
Illustrations
David Woodroffe
Designed and produced by
Atlantic Europe Publishing
Printed in China by
WKT Company Ltd

Exploring the endangered rainforest 2nd Edition – Curriculum Visions
A CIP record for this book is available from the British Library.

Paperback ISBN 978 1 78278 071 7

Picture credits
The Earthscape Picture Library, except *ShutterStock* cover, p1, 2–3, 4–5 (main), 12, 15 (insets), 16–17, 18–19, 20–21, 22–23 (main), 24–25, 28–29 (background), 30–31; *Corbis* 28 (bottom left).

This product is manufactured from sustainable managed forests. For every tree cut down at least one more is planted.